House Moving Made Easy

A Guide to Help You Plan, Organize, Declutter and Create Joy in Your New Home

---

Insights on how to plan, organize, simplify, and declutter — reducing the stress of moving while opening the door to joy, comfort, and well-being in your new home.

by: Margarita Tzetzou

House Moving Made Easy

Cover Designed by: Nikolaos Alexandrou

ISBN: 978-618-88109-0-7

Publisher: Margarita-Anna Tzetzou

First edition, 2025

Disclaimer

This book is intended for informational and inspirational purposes only.

The author has made every effort to ensure the accuracy of information at the time of publication.

Readers are encouraged to adapt suggestions to their individual circumstances and seek professional advice where appropriate. The author and publisher assume no responsibility for any loss, damage, or injury that may result from following the content of this guide.

Acknowledgements /Special Thanks:

To **OpenAI's ChatGPT**, an unexpected but steady ally in refining the language and tone of these pages — and for the many pearls of encouragement that helped me see my writing reflected back with clarity.

To **Kostandinos**, for selling me his apartment — not only did I gain a beautiful home filled with light, but I was also embraced by his wonderful family living on the other floors. I found both a home and a sense of belonging.

To **Maria**, the real estate agent, to whom I said, "If it's meant to be, then it will be." She saw how much I wanted this place to become my home and went the extra mile to make it happen.

To **Aliki**, the amazing and brilliant lawyer who, at first, gently warned me that it would be a huge task — and then, when I insisted this was *the* home for me, somehow made the impossible possible.

To **Mr. Nikos, his sons-and all the incredible Moving Team**, whose professionalism, good humor, and efficiency turned a potentially stressful process into a smooth moving experience.

To **Aggeliki**, a gentle angel soul, whose boundless love and generosity uplift everyone around her. She shares her discoveries and insights with infectious enthusiasm, always wishing the best for those she loves.

To **Katerina,** whose pragmatic support, sharing of positive signs from the universe, and early enthusiasm for the book idea gave me the confidence to begin writing it. Her kindness, generosity, and faith in me are lighthouse qualities that help me navigate through challenging times.

To **Nasline**, my sista and kindred spirit — ever my mirror in heart and humor. She's got my back as I have hers, and as a fellow writer, she immediately embraced the idea of this guidebook and cheered it on with love.

To **Anastasia** and "all the village" — my son's godmother and my psyche's confidant. Her playfulness and curiosity in exploring the meanderings of the mind are contagious. She is my daily diary, the one with whom I share the happenings, thoughts, and small triumphs (and challenges) of each day. Kind, giving, and steadfast — she has been there through many life events and both moves, caring for my son, cheering me on, and offering her ever-practical help with this book. Her presence is one of those rare blessings that make life gentler, brighter, and deeply grounded.

To **Philip**, **Evgenia and Andoni** — my dear brother, the "master declutterer" — for stepping in to help precisely when I need it most and for all his and Evgenia's valuable advice and support. For all their words of encouragement, good wishes and blessings.

To **my Mum**, thank you for pulling strings in heaven to help make this home a reality and for funding the refurbishments. The seahorse mosaic we created together is a cornerstone of our new space — you are with us always, and your love, creativity, and spirit live on, in our hearts.

And to **my gorgeous, most precious treasure — my son**, my sunshine, whose very existence *'en-lightens'* mine.

Table of contents:

Chapter 1

Acknowledging the Stress and Setting Intentions

Let's be honest — moving can feel like a daunting task, full of ups and downs. One moment you're buzzing with excitement, swept up in dreams of new beginnings, picturing fresh paint colors or imagining how your couch will look in the new space; the next, you're staring at a mountain of boxes wondering how on earth your life multiplied into so much stuff. And yes — it *is* super stressful.

Actually according to some studies it is considered as one of the most stressful life experiences ranked even above childbirth. In my opinion, having had a baby, having gone through the loss and grief of my mother's passing and moving yet again from having lived with my mother in a big apartment to a smaller one, all within a three year period – I would say that they are all equally stressful! It's just that each one tugs and exerts on the heart, the mind, the physical body, the practicalities, the finances and so on, on different levels.

The common thread that all life events have, is **Change**.

The ancient Greek philosopher, Heraclitus, said that "change is the only constant in life". He is also known for the quote "ta panta rei", meaning that "everything flows/everything is transient", like the water in a river.

There is no "perfect" move. However in the ensuing pages, I wish to impart insight so that that your move is more flowing. Being more aware of what to expect, bumps and all, you will be able to navigate a smoother moving experience.

The thing about moving is that it is not just about boxes and tape. You're not just packing objects; you're packing memories, routines, and pieces of a life you've built, leaving familiar surroundings and perhaps even familiar faces behind. There are also practical changes, like adapting to a new environment, building new social networks, and potentially altering one's daily routines and lifestyle.

Before stepping fully into a new space, it can be powerful to pause and acknowledge the home you are leaving behind. Every wall, every corner, every window has quietly held a part of your story. That home may have sheltered you in times of need, celebrated milestones with you, or simply offered the steady rhythm of daily life.

Taking a moment to express appreciation honours that history: gratitude for the lessons learned, the comfort received, and the memories created within those walls. I encourage you to begin this process as soon as you decide to move, rather than waiting until the final day when the moving truck is packed and ready to go. By saying goodbye gradually, from the very beginning, you gently and energetically detach from the space. This creates room for clarity, making it easier to shift into the practical and logical tasks of packing, organizing and choosing to release the items that no longer serve you.

There is no single right way to say goodbye, but here is a simple example you can use or adapt to honour your own parting:

I thank this home for its shelter.

I honour the memories it has held.

With gratitude, I release what has been.

With peace, I say goodbye.

And then, with that sense of completion, comes the invitation to step forward. Whatever the reason for moving on—growth, change, opportunity, or necessity—this new home represents the next stage of your unfolding journey. To enter it with awareness is to honour both past and future: carrying the essence of where you've been, while opening yourself fully to where you are going.

Once you have said your goodbyes, the next step is to welcome your new home with clear intentions and a sense of enthusiasm. This is the time to decide what you want your space to hold for you — not only emotionally, but physically. Consider the changes you'd like to make, whether it's updating plumbing or electrics, refreshing the bathroom or kitchen, or simply giving the walls a new coat of paint. Practical adjustments made now will save you stress later. If larger renovations are needed, it is wise to complete them before you move in; kitchens and bathrooms in particular can be disruptive, messy, and time-consuming projects once the house is occupied.

When working with contractors, make sure they can commit to a clear timeline so you're not moving into an unfinished space. Keep in mind that costs often rise along the way, so allow a buffer in your budget for unexpected "extras." If finances are tight, resist the urge to take on too much at once. Even small changes — such as painting walls yourself, refreshing fixtures, or adding personal touches — can dramatically shift the energy of the space and make it feel like yours from the beginning. This stage is about laying both the physical and energetic foundations for the life you want to grow here.

Just as there are many ways to say goodbye, there are also many ways to welcome a new home. Here is one simple example you can use or adapt to set your intentions as you step into this fresh chapter:

I welcome this home with joy and gratitude.

I fill its rooms with light and possibility.

May it be a space where life blossoms,

and where the best of me can unfold.

Here, I open the door to fresh beginnings.

Chapter 2

Getting Organized Before You Begin

This period can feel like a see-saw—an in-between stage with one foot still in the old home and the other already stepping into the new. Think of Janus, the Roman god of transitions (after whom January is named), with one face looking back and the other looking forward.

If your new place is far away, much of the preparation—arranging logistics, booking services, and tying up details—will happen online or by phone. It's time-consuming, yes, but because you're handling things remotely, you'll have more uninterrupted time to focus on packing.

If, on the other hand, you're moving within the same city, expect plenty of back-and-forth. This is especially true if you plan to revamp the new space and need contractors—plumbers, electricians, painters, and the like. There will be shopping trips for tiles, fixtures, or paint, meetings with tradespeople, and the inevitable round of gathering quotes. The latter is crucial: prices can vary enormously, and you'll want to strike the right balance between what truly needs doing (not just what you're told must be done) and what you're prepared to spend. Always add an extra 20–30% to your budget for the inevitable surprises—because they will come.

This kind of move is much more time-intensive, so keep it in mind when setting your moving date. If the date is fixed, be realistic about what can actually be achieved in the time available.

If you're moving within the same city, here's an idea I used in my last move: split it into two stages. It might sound unusual, but for me it was far more manageable. I had a lot of items to bring back from storage, plus many boxes already packed, and there simply wasn't space to stack more. So, I asked the moving company for two quotes—one for moving everything at once, and another for splitting it into two trips a couple of weeks apart. The total cost was the same, just spread into two installments.

In the first move, we transported the bulky furniture—couches, cupboards—and all the boxes I had already packed or retrieved from storage. That gave me time and space to finish packing the rest. The second move then handled the beds, kitchen supplies, appliances, and the remaining boxes.

Don't be afraid to suggest a similar arrangement with your movers. Thinking outside the box (pun intended) might give you a smoother, more bite-sized move that fits your needs.

Key Takeaways Before You Begin

- Plan early — book movers and tradespeople ahead of time
- If renovating or redecorating, allow extra time and add 20–30% to your budget for surprises.
- Get multiple quotes; don't just go with the first recommendation
- If moving locally, consider splitting the move into two stages for less stress and better flow.
- Keep flexibility in your schedule — unexpected tasks always appear.
- Think "outside the box": adapt the plan to your own rhythm and resources.

Creating a Balanced Realistic Timeline

Timeline for Work in Your Future Home

When setting up a timeline for your move, start by checking what needs to be done in the new home before you move in. Make a clear list: is it just painting, or are you looking at bigger projects like refurbishing a bathroom or kitchen? The scope of work will shape your timeline.

Next, decide how you want the work handled:

- **Separate contractors for each job** – This is usually less expensive, but it takes more time. Contractors often juggle multiple projects, so you may face delays while they finish other work or wait for things like drying or delivery of materials.

- **One full-service company or contractor** – This costs more, but it's quicker and more coordinated. The main drawback is that these companies often have waiting lists, so check their availability early.

As a rule of thumb, if you're doing major work (kitchen + bathroom + painting + floors), ***allow up to six months***. It might feel excessive, but it's realistic once you factor in delays, scheduling, and the order in which jobs need to be completed.

Tip: Build in a buffer of extra time, so if something runs late, you're not forced to move into an unfinished home.

Choosing Between Separate Contractors and One-Stop Shops

Personally, I prefer working with separate contractors. The "one-stop shop" approach usually means you have to buy all materials directly from them. While they might offer a decent selection, it's often limited to their style and taste, and the prices are usually much higher than what you'd find on the open market.

When working with separate contractors, be aware that not all of them provide written contracts—sometimes it's just an oral agreement covering the scope of work and payment terms. Always clarify exactly what materials are included in their fee. For instance, a plumber's fee usually covers the pipes within the wall, but fixtures such as taps, shower heads, and on/off valves are often the homeowner's responsibility. On the subject of plumbing, insist on copper pipes rather than plastic ones. While they cost more, they are far more hygienic, as mold cannot settle in their joints and crevices—an unseen issue that can affect your health through drinking water or even bathing.

A helpful practice is to keep a dedicated notebook with separate sections for each contractor. Since you may not have a formal contract, write down what's been agreed upon: the tasks, the payment amount, and the estimated time of completion (always add extra time to be realistic). Whenever you make a down payment or installment, have the contractor sign under the noted amount. This way, you maintain a clear record of what has been paid and what remains outstanding. And finally, never pay the full amount upfront—release payments gradually as the work progresses. Taking these steps keeps you protected, organized, and in control, even when formal contracts aren't in place.

By hiring separate contractors, you'll also take on the responsibility of sourcing the materials yourself. While this can be time-consuming, it opens the door to creativity and gives you access to a much wider range of options. You can shop around, look for specials, compare quality and even grab last pieces at bargain prices. Handled with a bit of planning, this part of the process can be both enjoyable and rewarding—your choices shape the character of your new home. One important detail: always check whether the material cost includes transportation. Some suppliers deliver directly to your front door, while others only drop items at the sidewalk. If it's the latter, you'll need to make sure your contractors are willing to bring everything inside—or, in trickier cases, arrange extra help. Think ahead about logistics such as whether there's a lift, whether the stairs are wide enough, or if you'll need special equipment (like an exterior truck lift to bring items through a balcony door).

Separate Contractors vs. One-Stop Shops: Pros and Cons

Here's a quick breakdown to help you compare both approaches at a glance:

Pros of Separate Contractors

- Wider range of materials and styles to choose from
- Ability to shop for deals, specials, and bargains
- More creative freedom to match your taste

Cons of Separate Contractors

- Time-consuming to source materials yourself
- More logistics to manage (deliveries, transportation, access)
- Greater need for coordination between different contractors

Pros of One-Stop Shops

- Convenience—everything (labor and materials) handled by one provider.
- No need for you to coordinate multiple contractors.
- Materials and services bundled together under one contract.

Cons of One-Stop Shops

- Limited selection tied to their suppliers and taste
- Higher material costs compared to market prices
- Less flexibility in customizing your choices

Timeline for Work in Your Future Home

Here's a practical guide to help you estimate how long different types of work may take, along with budget notes and key tips.

Timeline Guide	Budget Considerations	Tips and Notes
6 months (major works: kitchen + bathroom + painting + floors)	Separate contractors: usually cheaper, but slower due to juggling multiple projects and delivery delays.	Build in extra time to avoid moving into an unfinished home. Keep a clear list of all tasks in order.
4 months (medium works: bathroom OR kitchen + painting)	One-stop shops: more expensive, but progress is faster and more coordinated.	Check availability early—many full-service companies have waiting lists.
2–3 months (smaller works: painting, floors, light refurbishments)	With separate contractors, costs vary but can be controlled by shopping for your own materials.	Clarify what's included in fees (plumber's fixtures, electrician's fittings, etc.). Use a notebook to track tasks, payments, and timelines.

Timeline Guide	Budget Considerations	Tips and Notes
2–6 weeks (minor cosmetic updates only)	One-stop shops may not be worth the extra cost for very small projects.	Paying in installments is safer than paying upfront. Insist on copper pipes over plastic for plumbing.
Any timeline	Material transport may add costs—some suppliers deliver curbside only.	Plan logistics in advance: check stair width, lifts, or whether special equipment (like an exterior truck lift) is needed.

Realistic Timeline for Prepping in Your Current Home

Start by looking at the big picture: decide what furniture is coming with you and what isn't. Does the new home have space for everything? If not, the layout of your new space will naturally dictate what you can keep, sell, donate, or place in storage. From there, move on to smaller items—books, records, collections, and keepsakes. These are often the most time-consuming because they require careful sorting, and they also determine how many boxes you'll need.

Realistically, you should allow at least eight weeks for this process. Those weeks fly by, and it's easy to find yourself surrounded by half-packed "leaning towers of Pisa." This is where a reliable professional moving service can be a real lifesaver.

Full-service movers bring speed and efficiency. They arrive with tools, bubble wrap, tape, and experience. It saves enormous time, but comes at a higher cost.

DIY moving is cheaper on paper, but requires more preparation, renting vans, sourcing boxes, and heavy lifting. Unless you have very little to move, it can quickly become exhausting and physically demanding.

Hybrid moving is often the sweet spot. By packing your own boxes, you not only cut costs but also get the chance to declutter along the way. Movers can then focus on the heavy or fragile items—couches, beds, cupboards, appliances, and artwork. A good moving crew may even help with last-minute packing if you're running behind. From there, they'll load, transport, unload, and, if agreed in advance, reassemble furniture or unpack bulky items. Just make sure these extras are written into the contract from the beginning, as they often come with additional fees.

In this case, you'll need to purchase some supplies yourself:

- Cardboard boxes (various sizes): Avoid going for oversized boxes except for large items. For books, collectibles, and vinyl records (special LP boxes are usually 40x40), stick with smaller, more manageable sizes. They're easier to pack, carry, and stack without straining yourself. Also calculate extra boxes for the ones that will go to be sold or to charity.
- Clear plastic storage boxes: These are game changers—you can instantly see what's inside. They stack neatly and work well for seasonal clothing, toys, or anything you want to store in cupboards or on shelves.

- IKEA-style packing bags: Perfect for duvets, blankets, and clothing. They fold down flat when not in use, can be reused, and don't take up extra space.
- Heavy-duty garbage bags: They're useful for tossing in last-minute items such as laundry, and you'll need plenty of them on hand for the decluttering phase (covered in the following chapter)
- Good quality packing tape: Use the strong brown or clear tape for sealing boxes, and keep a few rolls of colored tape for easy room-by-room coding (e.g., kitchen, bathroom, bedroom, lounge, storage). Don't forget the white-and-red Fragile tape for delicate items.
- Masking tape: Great for securing bubble wrap without wasting expensive packing tape. It also doubles as a removable label for plastic boxes—handy if you want to reuse them later.
- Bubble wrap: Buy the 50-meter roll—it's cheaper and you'll likely use it all (you may even need more). Save it for your most delicate items, and use clothing or towels as extra padding where you can.
- Permanent markers: Essential for labeling the contents of each box.
- A folder or binder: Keep all receipts, contracts, and move-related paperwork in one place. Pair it with a

notebook—or your phone's notes app—for jotting down reminders, payment records, and important dates.

All of these supplies can easily be ordered online and delivered straight to your door. There's no need to wrestle with bulky packs of boxes or rolls of bubble wrap at the store and most of these items don't require close inspection before purchase. With the right supplies on hand, hybrid moving becomes far smoother, more organized, and far less stressful.

Other Important Considerations for Your Timeline and Budget

- **Air conditioners/HVAC units**: Uninstalling and reinstalling these requires a professional HVAC technician. It's not a DIY job — systems are sealed and complex. This service is costly and usually comes with waiting times, so book early and factor it into your budget. Also note that after re-installation, you will need another technician (servicing specialist) to service the units. This includes cleaning filters, coils, and fan blades with a strong antibacterial spray, checking electrical components, and verifying refrigerant levels. Regular servicing helps maintain energy efficiency, ensures healthy air quality, and reduces the risk of costly breakdowns later on. It's not as costly as the re-installation, but do budget for it, as the total can add up depending on how many units need servicing.

- **Cleaning services:** Budget for cleaning both homes. You'll likely need to leave your current place spotless for landlords, buyers, or the next occupants. At the same time, arrange for the new home to be cleaned before you move in—especially if renovations, painting, or refurbishments have left behind dust or debris. Post-renovation cleaning is usually more thorough (and sometimes more expensive) than standard cleaning.

- **Utility setup and disconnection:** Arrange utility setup in your new home well before the move. Contractors working on plumbing, electrical, or other renovations will need electricity and running water—tools aren't always battery-powered, and water must be on, to test for leaks. If you work remotely, having internet ready from the start avoids unnecessary downtime. On the other side, schedule utility shutoff in your current home for the day of the move or the following day. If you're moving out of town and a utility officer needs access, ask a neighbor or friend to be present.

Always take a photo of meter readings before leaving to prevent disputes or discrepancies on the final bill.

- **Professional storage expenses:** From experience, it's best to avoid putting items that don't fit into your new home straight into storage. What seems temporary often drags on much longer, and stored belongings can suffer damage despite careful packing. For example, a handmade Persian rug of mine was well-wrapped, yet moths still managed to get in and I had to throw it away. Storage facilities can also be vulnerable to issues like dampness, pests, or even floods. On top of that, access is often limited—you may need to file forms or wait for staff to retrieve boxes, which adds hassle.
  Another key factor is cost: monthly storage fees can add up quickly, sometimes becoming more expensive over a year than the value of what's being stored. Decluttering thoroughly before the move is usually the better option. If you have a basement, attic, or spare room in your new home, that can serve as a cost-free storage solution where you can access and integrate items at your own pace.

- **Disposal fees:** Bulky waste—like old mattresses, appliances, or furniture—often needs to be dealt with right around moving day. Some items can be picked up on the day of the move, while others may need to be handled shortly after, depending on what you've arranged with the disposal company. These pickups usually carry fees, but appliances can sometimes be cheaper to remove if they're going for recycling, since the company may receive a redemption. In some areas, the local municipality offers bulk-waste pickup, though you'll need to research availability and schedule a collection date in advance. If you're moving out of town, a trusted neighbor or friend can be invaluable for coordinating access for collection crews once you've left.

- **Sale & donate:** Selling items you no longer need can help offset moving costs, but be realistic in your expectations. Online listings may attract interest, but often from buyers in other cities who can't easily pick up the items. In practice, only local buyers who can collect in person are viable, which may limit sales. It's smart to have a backup plan: many charity organizations offer free pickups, but waiting lists can stretch up to two months, and they typically accept only items they believe they can resell. From experience, I found myself falling back on professional disposal services when sales didn't go through and charities declined certain items.

Timeline tip: Start the sale/donation process at least 8–10 weeks before moving day. This gives you time to attract local buyers, secure a slot with a charity if needed, and—if neither works out—still arrange for disposal services without a last-minute scramble.

- **Moving insurance:** Whether or not to purchase moving insurance depends largely on the type of move. For local or short-distance moves where you have control over the packing and transport, many people (myself included) find it an unnecessary expense. Professional movers typically take reasonable care, and damages are rare. However, for long-distance or international relocations—especially those involving containers, ships, or third-party handlers—insurance becomes much more important. The longer and more complex the journey, the greater the risk of loss or damage.

  Budgeting tip: Compare the cost of insurance against the replacement value of your most fragile or valuable items. If the premium is close to what replacement would cost, it may not be worth it. But if you're moving high-value items like antiques, instruments, or artwork, insurance could save you from a much larger expense in the unlikely event of damage.

- **Logistics:** Confirm in advance how far the movers will deliver—some bring items right into your home, while others unload only at the curb. Check whether stairways are wide enough and if elevators are both large and strong enough to handle bulky or heavy furniture. If not, special equipment such as an exterior lift or crane may be required, which adds both time and cost.

  Also be aware that some municipalities require you to notify them of your moving date, the streets involved, and potential disruptions if a truck or van will be blocking the road. In many cases, they'll insist that you mark off the space the day before using red-and-white tape with a posted notice stating that no one should park there during specific hours. This ensures the moving truck has space to park and unload safely, and saves you from last-minute stress—or even fines—on moving day.

- **Day-of Move - hospitality:** It may go without saying, but budget for coffee, water, or light snacks for your movers. Depending on the size of the move, more crew members may show up than you expect, so plan a little extra—no one likes a cheapskate. Small gestures like this keep morale high, set a cooperative tone, and are almost always repaid in goodwill and extra care with your belongings. If friends are helping instead, consider ordering pizza or another easy meal once everything is unloaded. It's a simple but thoughtful way to thank them and to celebrate the first evening in your new home.

- **Childcare & pet care:** Moving day is stressful enough without having to constantly check where your children or pets are. Ideally, plan the move during school hours or ask a trusted family member or close friend to look after them—providing meals, entertainment, and supervision—so you can stay fully focused on the tasks at hand. Another creative option is to have a friend take them to a park, indoor play center, or other activity to keep them happily occupied.

  Trust is key: children and pets are your most precious treasures, so only leave them with someone you can rely on completely. If that's not possible, you'll need to keep them nearby and ensure they have food, water, bathroom breaks, and a safe space to rest while the move is underway. The same principle applies to pets—

arrange for someone you trust to walk, feed, or watch them, or set up a quiet room away from the chaos to keep them calm and secure.

With these pieces in place, your current home will be ready in good time, your move will run more smoothly, and you'll avoid last-minute stress and surprise costs.

Realistic Timeline for Prepping in Your Current Home

Use this guide to structure the weeks before your move, keep your budget realistic, and stay on top of key tasks.

Timeline Guide	Budget Considerations	Tips and Notes
10–8 weeks before move	Budget for donation pickups, disposal fees, or storage if needed. Selling items locally saves costs, but may not always work. Charity pickups are free but can have 6–8 week wait times. Disposal services have fees.	Start the sale/donate/dispose process early to avoid last-minute costs. Have a backup plan in case sales or donations don't work out. Avoid rushing last minute.
8 weeks before move	Compare costs of DIY vs. hybrid vs. full-service movers.	Order packing supplies online (boxes, tape, bubble wrap, IKEA bags, plastic bins). Hybrid moving often offers the best balance of cost and control.
6 weeks before move	Factor in costs for HVAC removal/reinstallation if needed. Budget for the Servicing Technician as well, the total can add up depending on how many units need servicing	Confirm any large items that require disassembly or special handling. Start packing seasonal or rarely used items. Book HVAC services early due to waiting lists. Book also the service technician who will come after the re-installation to clean filters and top up refrigerant.

Timeline Guide	Budget Considerations	Tips and Notes
4 weeks before move	Book cleaning services for both homes (post-renovation cleaning costs more).	Arrange utility setup in your new home. Take photos of meter readings before disconnecting utilities in the current home.
3 weeks before move	If considering storage, weigh monthly fees vs. item value.	Avoid long-term storage if possible—items can get damaged or forgotten. Declutter instead.
2 weeks before move	Plan disposal pickups for bulky items (mattresses, appliances, furniture).	Confirm moving insurance if doing a long-distance or international move.
1 week before move	Budget for hospitality (coffee, water, snacks, or pizza for movers/friends). Confirm arrangements for Childcare/Pet care	Confirm logistics with movers—stair size, elevators, parking permits, special equipment if needed.
The day before move	Possible small municipal fee if reserving curbside space.	Research municipal rules for reserving a truck space. Post red & white tape & notice the day before to block parking.

Timeline Guide	Budget Considerations	Tips and Notes
Day of move	Hospitality for movers/friends (snacks, coffee, pizza). Childcare/Pet care (professional or trusted family/friends)	Keep children and pets safe and cared for away from the chaos. Be ready with Payment of the movers and tips for the crew if any. Have with you contracts, receipts, and moving paperwork in a dedicated folder. Take meter photos before leaving.

Chapter 3

Decluttering with Purpose

Oh boy – I face the same struggle getting started with decluttering, whether in real life or on paper.

When I ask myself why it feels so hard, I realize my brain immediately pictures all the stuff at once, and suddenly climbing Mount Everest seems like the easier task. In truth, decluttering does take time, effort, and energy. It's tiresome and cumbersome. But once you get the ball rolling — sorting and packing into piles for keeping, donating, selling, or tossing into those big black garbage bags (which fill up surprisingly fast) — then bam! It's like slaloming down Everest, having already conquered our baggage: old versions of ourselves, past traumas, and that persistent 'just in case' mindset. What remains is a sovereign inner space where you've done the shadow work, know who you are, and no longer let objects define you. Here, only the essentials remain — the items precious to heart and soul, adding either beauty or function to your new home. So, how do we get there? In the following pages, I'll share what I've discovered, what I've come to understand more deeply, and the tips that make that downhill run liberating.

Before diving into the nitty-gritty of decluttering, start with the bigger picture — the furniture. Look at the dining table, bookcases, sofas, and other large pieces, and consider what will truly fit into your new home. The space itself defines what you can keep. If something won't fit, no longer serves a purpose, or simply doesn't feel right anymore, see if friends or family might want it, or take photos and list it for sale.

For instance, there was no space for a third couch in my new home, and the dining table was far too big for the room. While chatting with my son's godmother, she mentioned she had a dining table in storage and wanted to replace her old one — which turned out to be the perfect size for me. She also needed a larger couch, so we swapped: I gave her the couch, she gave me the dining table, and I sold my old one. A true win–win situation

For this recent home move, I had to declutter not only my own belongings but also all the possessions of my mother who had passed on. It felt like an insurmountable task — every nook and cranny, every drawer, every cupboard was crammed full of things.

Different objects trigger different responses, so I decided to start with bite-sized tasks and easier categories — like **books.** Small boxes are best (they get heavy quickly):

one box to keep and one to give away. I'd grab a pile from the shelf and ask myself: Will I re-read this? Is it a useful reference? Is it a classic a younger family member might enjoy one day? If yes, it went into the keep box. On the other hand, if the book had already served its purpose — for example, candle-making guides, mosaics, hanging basket, how-tos, or travel books about places I've already visited and won't return to (that 'been there, done that' feeling) — it went into the give-away box.

I did, however, make one big mistake. My brother, who I call the master declutterer — with laser focus and the ability to tear through piles, filling black garbage bags at lightning speed — warned me there would be no place for encyclopedias. He was right. With so much available online, I thought they might still come in handy, but now I can't even recycle them without paying for it. Mistakes happen, but that's how we learn.

Next, I moved on to the old **photo albums** — the kind that hold entire family histories: parents, grandparents, and the toddler version of yourself. At some point, you may have set the intention to scan them for a digital record, but for now, they go straight into the keep box. Happy memories or not, these are irreplaceable pieces of our past. As the saying goes, a picture is worth a thousand words, and photographs have the remarkable power of time travel — instantly transporting us back to a moment long gone.

Photos can also serve as a kind of 'response gauge.' For those who've experienced a difficult or traumatic childhood, images may still trigger pain. If they do, it's a sign the wound remains open and more healing work is needed — shadow work that transforms the wound into a scar. A scar means the memory is still there, but it no longer holds power over you. Sometimes, photos can even become tools in therapy: a way to voice your hurt and anger, or, if necessary, to physically tear them up as part of a healing process.

After working through the albums — a process that touched both memory and heart — I was ready to return to something more tangible and less emotionally charged. The next category I tackled was trinkets and bibelots, those porcelain ornaments and little treasures that seem to multiply on every shelf and, like desert water collectors, somehow manage to draw dust out of thin air in record time.

Of course, **trinkets** come with their own challenge — they're fragile. This is where the bubble wrap comes in (and runs out far too quickly), leaving you padding them with T-shirts or bits of clothing to keep them safe in the box.

My mum had such a lovely decorative knack — nothing in her home ever looked excessive. She always found a spot for everything, so it never felt like she was hoarding. She collected bibelots, tea sets, dinner services, and fine cutlery. Even though I had already sorted and sold many items two years earlier — a process she found difficult, as letting go didn't come easily to her — there were still what felt like a gazillion ornaments and enough tableware to furnish four homes. This time, I kept only the pieces I loved most and sold the rest at giveaway prices.

After her passing, I came to understand something deeper about her attachment to those objects. My parents had immigrated and were unable to bring much with them; my mother had to leave behind her entire wedding trousseau — beautiful dinnerware, tea sets, and cherished gifts. When she later returned for her parents' funerals, she discovered that everything she had left behind was gone — her possessions, her parents' things, all of it. Only one or two items remained.

Her parents had hosted huge family gatherings — seven or eight families at a time — filled with warmth, laughter, and elaborate meals: hors d'oeuvres, starters, mains, cheeses, fruit, desserts, nuts, and liqueurs. I believe that, subconsciously, she tried to recreate those feelings of safety, belonging, and home by accumulating enough dinnerware and cutlery to serve a crowd. She did host large gatherings when I was young, but over time, as life changed, these dwindled down to smaller family dinners.

During the decluttering process, it's worth reflecting on whether similar subconscious patterns exist within ourselves — habits or emotional imprints from childhood that make us collect certain items or struggle to release what no longer serves our present lives.

Next, I turned my attention to the **kitchenware**. Once again, there was an abundance — bowls, Pyrex dishes, flan tins, serving plates, and more — scattered across different cupboards. I wasn't quite sure where to start or how to decide what to keep and what to let go of.

Just then, my brother popped round. Within minutes, he had emptied every cupboard, spreading everything out in neat rows across the floor: all the Pyrex in one line, glass bowls in another, flan and pie dishes in the next, pots and pans in separate rows, and jugs with serving utensils grouped together. Suddenly, I had a clear bird's-eye view of everything — and it was instantly obvious where the duplicates and triplicates were hiding.

I certainly didn't need three glass mixing bowls of the exact same size. The only items I allowed myself to keep more than one of were the casserole dishes — they're versatile, sturdy, and rare to find pieces that work both on the stove and in the oven. Besides, they come in handy when serving several dishes at once.

That little exercise was such a game-changer. That visual clarity made all the difference. What could have taken me hours was obvious in minutes. If you find yourself with multiple items serving the same purpose — not just in the kitchen, but anywhere — laying them all out together can bring instant perspective and make choosing (and releasing) so much easier.

Next came the **bathroom**. Inevitably, there were countless little bottles, creams, shampoos, and shower gels tucked away everywhere. This area, however, was surprisingly straightforward — most of those bottles went straight into one of the big black garbage bags.

Most creams and toiletries have a shelf life of about six months once opened, yet somehow we all keep products that have long gathered dust. Often, they didn't suit our skin or we simply didn't like them, but we hang onto them thinking we might give them another try — though deep down, we know we won't. Many of these items were also expensive, and letting them go can feel like admitting we "wasted" money. But this is exactly where focus is needed: it's time to be firm and start tossing things into the bag — old scrubs, worn-out sponges and brushes, pumice stones, tiny soap remnants, outdated creams and bottles.

Keep only what you genuinely use: your regular shower gel and shampoo, and the face and body creams you truly reach for. The bathroom, in my view, is the one room in the home best kept minimalistic. When it's functional, fresh, and uncluttered, it instantly supports a positive frame of mind. This doesn't mean it should feel bare — I love the touch of plush towels, a few well-chosen toiletries neatly stored in a drawer, and just a handful of beautiful items on display to create that calm, spa-like atmosphere.

One little tip: replace your toothbrushes on moving day. Use the old ones in the morning before you leave, and start fresh with new ones when you arrive — it's a simple gesture that symbolizes a clean beginning.

Pack all the bathroom items you're taking in clear plastic boxes — you'll be able to see what's inside right away, making it one of the first boxes to unpack in your new home. Do the same for your medicines, whether they're kept in the bathroom or kitchen: check for expiry dates, leaks, and anything unnecessary. For cough syrups or children's medications, seal them in a zip bag on the day of the move before placing them in the box. Keep this box close at hand with your essentials, so your new home feels organized and functional from the very first day.

Decluttering even a small space like the bathroom can remind us that clarity and calm often begin in the simplest corners — when we release the excess, we make room for ease and renewal.

Next came the **tablecloths, dishcloths, and hand-sewn heirlooms** — a fairly simple section to sort through. With the heirlooms, I kept the ones I truly loved; the rest, though beautiful, could find new homes and even fetch a decent price. Often, we keep using the same old, worn tablecloths while the good ones — the ones we're "saving" for special occasions — sit folded at the bottom of a drawer. But moving into a new home is a special occasion. It's the perfect time to start enjoying what we already own. Even if a lovely tablecloth gets a stain or two, it's worth it for the joy of eating every meal beautifully set, celebrating each and every day.

Tablecloths, runners, and placemats can truly complement the furniture they sit on. They have a quiet way of transforming a table into a place of welcome. So, let go of the old, tired pieces. You deserve to enjoy the beauty and comfort of your best things every day, not only when guests come around.

The same goes for dishcloths and oven gloves: keep the good, sturdy cotton or linen ones. As for those synthetic microfiber kinds that make your fingertips cringe — I'd rather use the old cotton ones than those any day!

Then came the **linen** cupboard. There's nothing more delicious on the skin than crisp, smooth, high-thread-count (200–600) cotton sheets. They're durable, breathable, and timeless. If your sheets have those little fuzzed knots on them, they've seen better days. And while satin ones may look luxurious, they can feel slippery and stifling — like trying to sleep on silk pyjamas made of soap bubbles! The flannel ones, tend to cling — I jokingly call it the "Velcro effect." In winter, I sometimes layer a flannel sheet underneath the cotton ones for warmth, but never as the top layer.

If you don't yet own 100% cotton sheets, this is one investment truly worth making for your new home. Look for good-quality, high-thread-count ones — even plain designs are fine; what matters is how they feel. Pack all your existing sheets, pillowcases, and duvet covers into large, sturdy storage bags (Ikea-style ones are perfect). Keep one set of fresh, clean sheets ready to put straight onto your bed the first night — there's no better feeling than slipping into crisp sheets after a long moving day.

The same principle applies to towels. Keep the ones that still feel soft and absorbent, and say goodbye to any that have lost their plushness. I'm not a fan of those ultra-thick, hotel-style towels — they're heavy, take forever to dry, and strain the washing machine. The very thin ones, on the other hand, feel like drying off with blotting paper. Somewhere in between is the "Goldilocks" zone — just right. When you look at your towel cupboard, you'll instantly know which ones deserve to come with you and which have served their purpose. Keep a fresh set ready to go into the same bag as your first-night sheets.

One more thing to include in that bag: a set of curtains for the bedrooms. Trust me — from experience — don't overlook this detail. On our first night in the new home, I hadn't yet put up any curtains. I turned off the lights, slipped into my crisp, clean sheets feeling rather pleased with myself… until my three-year-old started crying. Even though the shutters were closed, the streetlights and passing cars cast moving shadows on the walls — everything was unfamiliar to him. I took him out onto the balcony to show him the lights and reassure him until he calmed down. The next morning, I rummaged through the storage bags to find the curtains and hung them up straightaway.

I had parted with many of our old curtains — some were faded, some I was simply tired of. I wanted something new to match the fresh energy of the home, and managed to find a lovely set on sale, which felt like a small victory. As the seasons change, I swap out lighter, summery ones for thicker, warmer ones — sometimes adapting or shortening an old pair, and occasionally treating myself to something new when the budget allows.

Soft furnishings carry the warmth of comfort and familiarity — choosing them mindfully helps your new home feel like you from the very first night.

Storage Areas: Attic, Basement, or Garage: Inevitably, these spaces become the catch-all zones for everything from Christmas trees and decorations to carpets, heaters, fans, tools, and half-used paint tins. Start by getting rid of old paints that are more than a few months opened. Anything that smells of mould or damp should go straight out; don't let those odours "contaminate" your new home's storage area.

Only take what's truly necessary and what you know will fit comfortably in your new home's storage. Make sure everything you keep is clean, dry, and well-wrapped for the move. Christmas decorations can go neatly into clear plastic boxes — they'll stay dust-free, waterproof, and you'll instantly see what's inside next year.

This is also where I found myself discarding mountains of forgotten things: tangled cables, a rusty drying rack, old metal folding bed, paintbrushes gone stiff, worn-out backpacks, and mountains of shoes. Speaking of shoes

— we all tend to keep pairs that hurt, ones that used to be comfortable but are now past their prime, or those brand-new ones that never quite fit (and our feet still remember the blisters!). I gave away a gazillion pairs, some brand new still in their boxes. I realized that after pregnancy, my shoe size and shape had changed — so I kept only the ones that fit perfectly, Cinderella-style. Be brave; you'll surely find items that no longer serve their purpose. Throw away, recycle, or give to charity.

Every shelf you empty and box you sort through is a quiet reclaiming of order and calm.

Next — **children's toys, books, and all their paraphernalia**. Moving is the perfect opportunity to donate those outdated baby toys and books — but only if your child has truly outgrown them. If they've been long forgotten, the process will be much easier. And if your child has already seen you giving away boxes of things you no longer need, you're setting a wonderful example — teaching by doing.

However, here's the thing: <u>you have to ask them</u>. My greatest faux pas was giving away my toddler's baby toys without checking first. He had already accumulated so many new ones that I assumed he wouldn't notice. But I was wrong. When all his toys were unpacked in the new home, he looked around for his old, bulky wooden pull-along train — the one I'd unknowingly given to charity. I called the charity a few days later, but the toys had already been passed on.

I apologized, explaining that I should have asked him first, and then took him shopping for a new, more modern train — even though our post-move budget was tight. The experience reminded me of a story my mother had shared years ago: how her own mother had given away her doll to a cousin without asking. It had hurt her deeply, though she never spoke of it at the time. That small act had left a lasting imprint — perhaps even explaining her later reluctance to let go of things.

I can only hope I haven't created any lasting hurt for my boy. But I believe that acknowledging it, apologizing, and making amends showed him that his feelings matter — that his voice counts.

Lastly, the **clothes**... These tend to fall into a few familiar categories — seasonal, formal, the "too small but maybe one day" items, and the regular, comfy clothes we reach for every day.

Here again, I used a mix of IKEA storage bags and clear plastic boxes so I could easily see what was inside — along with a healthy dose of honesty. You don't need every outfit from yesteryear, nor all those smaller-sized clothes you plan to fit into someday. Keep only a few sentimental or timeless pieces that never go out of style — and limit them to one bag or box.

I began with the formal wear. Usually, there aren't too many pieces here — keep the classics that don't date, and place the rest in a large black garbage bag for charity or a vintage shop.

Next came the winter clothes, which are bulky and a bit awkward to pack. I used IKEA storage bags for coats and jackets, checking all the pockets (you never know what forgotten treasures might be hiding there!). Keep the ones that fit well and are still in good shape. If something's faded, missing buttons, or has a broken zipper, decide whether to repair it — if you have a better version, let it go. Once clean and refreshed, pack everything neatly into the storage bags so it's ready to use when the cold season returns.

As for jerseys, I gave away many — I had far too many to begin with! The ones I kept, I rolled and placed in plastic boxes. Rolling saves space and makes it easy to spot each one later when the seasons change.

Summer clothes, on the other hand, are light and easy — roll them up and you'll be amazed how much fits into a single plastic box.

Whichever season you're currently in, leave that wardrobe for last. About a week before the move, pack most of it, keeping aside roughly two weeks' worth of fresh clothes. (I suggest two weeks because you may need time to get your washing machine reinstalled and running — I had arranged for a technician to come the very afternoon of the move so I could get laundry sorted right away.)

For the laundry, I used a simple system: a large garbage or IKEA blue carrier bag for dirty clothes packed on moving day (I avoided the storage bags here to prevent confusion with the clean items), and a separate laundry bag for clean clothes that still needed ironing.

Let your wardrobe reflect who you are now — comfortable in your skin, confident in your choices, and happy knowing that you wear your clothes, not the other way around.

The way I see it, moving house, holds so many opportunities for change: for releasing what no longer serves, both the inner and the outer luggage, for giving items to charity or people that most need them, for selling items if you can, basically going in 'lighter' into your new home. In truth, less is more.

If you are able to declutter objects essentially, you are more likely to be able to 'declutter' what people say as well, keeping what is of importance and letting go of the rest.

This reminds me of a quote by Dinah Maria Mulock Craik, In this decluttering instance I am going to use it inter alia for objects and people.

"Oh, the comfort, the inexpressible comfort of feeling safe with a person; having neither to weigh thoughts nor measure words, but to pour them all out, just as they are, chaff and grain together, knowing that a faithful hand will take and sift them, keep what is worth keeping, and then, with a breath of kindness, blow the rest away."

So, as you declutter, remember - Be gentle as you let go, graceful as you begin anew, and let your home become the echo of your heart - a space where kindness lingers, memories rest softly, and new dreams take root.

Decluttering with Purpose — Summary of Insights & Practical Strategies

The following table gathers the most valuable insights, reflections, and practical steps from this chapter — a quick reference guide to help you stay grounded, intentional, and inspired throughout your own decluttering journey.

Category / Area	Core Insight or Reflection	Practical Tips & Strategies
Mindset & Approach	Decluttering isn't just physical —it's emotional and symbolic. Releasing items helps release the past and make room for renewal.	Start small (bite-sized areas). Sort into clear piles: *keep, donate, sell, discard*. Use manageable boxes or bags. Celebrate progress, not perfection.
Furniture & Large Items	Your new home's space defines what you can keep — let the home's energy guide your choices.	Measure rooms beforehand. Offer unwanted pieces to friends/family. Sell via online listings. Collaborate — creative exchanges can benefit both parties.
Books & Paper Items	Books mirror phases of life — keep only those that inform or inspire your present and future self.	Sort in small boxes: one to keep, one to give away. Keep classics or meaningful references; release the rest. Avoid keeping encyclopedias or outdated reference sets.

Category / Area	Core Insight or Reflection	Practical Tips & Strategies
Photos & Memorabilia	Photos connect us to the past; they can also reflect our emotional healing journey.	Keep originals for scanning later. If certain images trigger pain, use them for gentle self-reflection or healing exercises.
Trinkets & Bibelots	Sentimental collections often echo past emotional needs — awareness brings release.	Keep only those that spark joy or meaning. Use bubble wrap or soft fabrics for packing. Sell or donate excess.
Kitchenware	Visual clarity transforms decision-making — seeing everything together exposes duplicates instantly.	Lay out all items by category (bowls, pots, dishes). Keep versatile, quality pieces. Limit duplicates. Use clear labeling and sturdy boxes.
Bathroom & Toiletries	A minimal bathroom supports mental clarity - freshness equals calm.	Discard expired products. Keep only daily essentials. Replace toothbrushes on moving day for a symbolic fresh start. Use clear boxes for toiletries and medicines.

Category / Area	Core Insight or Reflection	Practical Tips & Strategies
Table Linens & Soft Furnishings	Everyday beauty matters — you deserve to use your best, not save it for guests.	Keep good-quality cotton or linen items. Let go of worn pieces. Use elegant tablecloths and runners to elevate daily meals.
Bedding & Towels	Quality over quantity enhances comfort and wellbeing.	Invest in high-thread-count cotton sheets (200–600). Keep towels in the “Goldilocks” range — not too thick, not too thin. Prepare a “first-night” set of sheets, towels and curtains.
Curtains	Curtains offer both comfort and emotional security especially for children.	Keep a set ready for the first night. Choose new or refreshed curtains that match your home’s new vibe. Swap seasonally for warmth or lightness.

Category / Area	Core Insight or Reflection	Practical Tips & Strategies
Storage Areas (Attic/ Basement/ Garage)	Storage should not be a dumping ground — only what serves your life should move forward.	Discard mouldy items or old paints. Clean and dry everything. Store Christmas Décor in clear boxes. Give away unused items, cables, and old shoes. Keep only what fits and functions.
Children's Toys & Books	Decluttering with kids teaches empathy, responsibility, and respect for their feelings.	Involve children in the process — always ask before donating their things. Model generosity. Use decluttering, as life lessons in choice, gratitude, and autonomy.
Clothing	Let your wardrobe mirror your present self — confident, authentic, and comfortable.	Sort by category: seasonal, — formal, — sentimental. Use clear boxes and storage bags. Keep only what fits well and feels good. Pack two weeks of clothes for the move. Donate or recycle the rest.

Category / Area	Core Insight or Reflection	Practical Tips & Strategies
Emotional Reflection	Decluttering, mirrors inner work — letting go of what no longer serves, allows peace to take root.	Be kind to yourself through the process. Keep what uplifts you, release the rest with gratitude. Approach each space with calm and compassion.
Overall Closing Wisdom	"Less is more" — both in possessions and in emotional weight. A lighter home nurtures inner and outer spaciousness.	As you declutter, be gentle in letting go, graceful in beginning anew, and let kindness and intention guide each choice.

Chapter 4

Packing Smarter and Gearing towards the Move

Leading on from the previous chapter, once you're well on your way with decluttering and the packing process, take a moment to plan how you'll label and track your boxes. A little organization now will save a great deal of time and confusion later.

Start by clearly writing what each box contains — be specific, as this will make unpacking easier and help you decide what to open first. I prefer to number each box and jot down its contents in a notebook or notepad *only* if it's going to be a long-distance move or if items are going by container or shipping. That way, you know exactly how many boxes there are in total and can do a quick reconciliation upon arrival. However, if you'll be present during both the loading and unloading, that extra step may not be worth the time.

Now, what I'm truly a fan of is colour coding! Assign a colour to each room using coloured tape or stickers. There's no need to go overboard with too many categories — just stick to the basics. Since coloured tape isn't cheap, use moderate-sized pieces on the top and two sides of each box so they're visible when stacked. It's a small effort that makes a big difference: when unloading, you'll instantly know where everything belongs. For example:

- Red for the living area or lounge
- Green for the kitchen
- Blue for the bathroom, and so on.

If you're using clear plastic boxes, the contents are already visible, but it's still useful to place a small coloured label or piece of tape on the top for the movers' quick reference.

If you're opting for a hybrid mode — doing some packing yourself and having movers assist — then you can organize and colour code your boxes exactly as you wish. However, if professional movers are handling all the packing, ask them from the outset how they label boxes and whether they offer a colour-coding system (and if it comes at an extra cost). That way, you'll have a clear plan and budget from the start.

It goes without saying that boxes containing fragile items should be clearly marked as such. Use "FRAGILE" tape all around the box — this is one area where you don't want to be subtle. Make sure it's visible from every angle so movers can't miss it. Inside the box, wrap delicate pieces carefully in bubble wrap, or, as I often do, use clothes, tablecloths, or dishcloths as padding — they're practical, space-saving, and surprisingly effective.

Also, plan ahead for how you'll handle your most important or valuable items — your "holy of holies." Think jewellery, passports, tax records, family documents, and anything else you simply can't afford to lose. If you have a trusted family member or friend nearby, consider taking these items to them a day or two before the move for safekeeping until you're settled.

If that's not an option, keep them close at hand on moving day — either in your handbag, backpack, or a clearly marked box that never leaves your sight. You can even mark that box with multiple colours of tape and a strip of fragile tape for good measure, so you instantly recognise it as your most important one.

Items to remember as you gear up for the move:

If your fridge requires defrosting, plan for it at least one to two weeks before moving day. You don't want to spend your last few hours mopping up melted ice! I defrosted mine a week before and made sure we used up everything in the freezer, avoiding big grocery shops in those final days — just the essentials to get by.

The night before the move, prepare easy snacks — fruit, sandwiches, and bottled water — for yourself and your family. On moving morning, pack all remaining perishables into a cooler bag with a few ice packs, and keep it in the fridge until the movers arrive. That way, it's quick to grab before the fridge gets packed up.

Once your fridge is placed in your new home, remember to let it "settle" for about two hours before plugging it in. This pause allows the refrigerant fluid to stabilize after transport — a small but important detail to ensure everything runs smoothly.

If you're moving long-distance or your belongings will be in transit for several days, locate the **transit bar** (the metal rod that originally came with your washing machine). It's probably stored in a cupboard or utility area near the machine. Make sure the movers refit it before transport — it keeps the drum securely in place and prevents internal damage during the journey.

Make arrangements with your electrician ahead of time, as only a certified professional can safely install your oven or stove, as well as any new light fixtures, plugs, or switches. I had mine on standby and called him as soon as the movers left — within an hour, the cooker was installed and the lights were up. It made such a difference to have the essentials ready right away.

Also, don't forget to buy the light bulbs you'll need in advance. Check both the brightness and the hue — I personally prefer the warmer tones that mimic natural sunlight, as they create a softer, more welcoming atmosphere. The cooler, bluish ones can feel a bit stark and less comforting — but that's entirely a matter of preference.

Another meaningful idea as you gear up for the move is to involve your family members in creating or choosing something specifically for the new home. This encourages emotional readiness and enthusiasm, helping everyone feel part of the transition. You might make something handmade together or allow each person to select a small item that will have a place in the new space. For example, my mother and I created a lovely seahorse mosaic from sea pebbles — a project that took us a couple of months, knowing it would one day adorn our new bathroom. She is no longer with me physically, but that piece feels like her blessing in our new home — a true masterpiece that fills the space with warmth, memory and beauty.

On the practical side — many of these points were touched upon in earlier chapters, but as the move draws closer, it's worth revisiting **your essentials** to ensure nothing slips through the cracks.

Start with your **cleaning plan**. Ideally, your new home should be cleaned before your belongings arrive. However, if that's not possible, ask your movers to leave the broom, mop, and bucket (complete with wipes, cloths, and bin bags) in an easily accessible area so you can do a quick clean before unpacking.

Notify all utility providers of your move-out and move-in dates, and make sure your post is redirected. Update your address with banks, insurance companies, and schools. On moving day, take photos of your utility meters for your records — it will make any later reconciliation much smoother.

Next, pack your **"First-Night Essentials Box" (or boxes)** — the real lifesavers for that first night and morning in your new home:

- **Bathroom kit:** toiletries, razor, hairbrush and dryer, new toothbrushes, fresh towels, and a bath mat.

- **Clothing and linens:** pyjamas, underwear, clothes for the first week or two, and your favourite bed linen — perfect for inaugurating your first night's sleep. Remember the bedroom curtains, too; they offer privacy and comfort, especially for children.

- **Tech and tools:** chargers, laptop, basic tools (including a Phillips and flat-head screwdriver), and scissors.

- **Health and personal needs:** medications and any daily essentials.

- **Kitchen basics:** kettle, toaster, mugs, glasses, plates, and cutlery. If you've packed your tableware in clear, colour-coded boxes, you'll know exactly where to find them. Otherwise, prepare a single "essentials" box with everything needed for that much-deserved first cup of tea or coffee — including tea, coffee, sugar or honey, cereal, and a few breakfast items.

- **For your pets:** food, water bowl, and any favourite toy or blanket to help them settle in.

If you have children or pets, **confirm care arrangements** for moving day. Having a trusted friend or family member look after them keeps everyone safe and allows you to focus. Keep their favourite snacks, toys, or blankets nearby — familiar comforts go a long way in easing the transition.

The day before the move, **reserve a parking space** for the movers' truck. You can cordon off the area with red-and-white tape between trees or poles and post a clear notice stating the date and hours of the move. (Check with your local municipality first if permission is required.)

The days leading up to a move can be busy and scattered, but preparation is what transforms chaos into calm. Each small step — labeling, planning, checking, double-checking — is really about something deeper: creating order out of change. And when moving day finally arrives, you'll find that you haven't just packed your belongings — you've packed peace of mind.

The following summary gathers the most practical reminders and thoughtful insights from this chapter — a checklist not just for efficiency, but for peace of mind. Think of it as your calm companion in the days leading up to the move — a way to keep track, stay grounded, and move forward with intention.

Table: Gearing Towards the Move – Key Reminders, Practical Steps, and Tips

Category / Area	Core Insight or Reflection	Practical Tips & Strategies
Family Readiness	Encourage emotional connection to the new home.	Invite family members—especially children—to make or choose something for the new space (e.g., artwork, small décor, plant). This builds excitement and a sense of belonging.
Cleaning & Preparation	Prepare for cleaning both homes before and after moving.	Ensure cleaning supplies (broom, mop, bucket, wipes, cloths, bin bags) are packed together and easily accessible before unloading begins. Budget for a deep clean if possible.
Utility Management	Avoid post-move administrative stress.	Notify utility providers of your move-out and move-in dates. Take photos of meter readings on moving day and update addresses with banks, insurance, schools, etc.

Category / Area	Core Insight or Reflection	Practical Tips & Strategies
Fridge & Appliances	Prevent last-minute mess or damage.	Defrost your fridge 1–2 weeks before moving. Use up frozen foods. Pack a cooler bag with ice packs for perishables on the day. After moving, wait at least 2 hours before plugging the fridge in.
Electrical Installations	Ensure safety and compliance.	Arrange for a certified electrician to install your cooker, oven, and lighting. Purchase bulbs in advance (warm light creates a cozy ambience).
Washing Machine Transport	Avoid internal damage.	Locate and re-install the stabilizing bar before transport if using long-distance shipping or containerized moving
Valuables & Documents	Prevent loss or damage of irreplaceable items.	Keep passports, jewellery, and essential documents in a personal bag or separate, clearly marked box (you may use all colour tapes plus "FRAGILE" tape for identification).

Category / Area	Core Insight or Reflection	Practical Tips & Strategies
Essential "First-Night" Box	Prepare boxes to cover basic needs for the first night and following day.	Pack labelled essentials by category: • Bathroom kit – toiletries, towels, toothbrushes, bath mat .• Bedroom kit – pyjamas, fresh bed linen, bedroom curtains. • Tech & tools – chargers, laptop, screwdriver, scissors. • Kitchen basics – kettle, mugs, breakfast items, pet supplies. • Medications and daily-use items.
Children & Pets	Reduce stress and ensure safety.	Arrange for childcare or pet care on moving day. Keep their favourite toys, snacks, or blankets close to provide comfort and familiarity.
Parking & Access	Smooth logistics for moving trucks.	Keep a set ready for the first night. Choose new Reserve parking for the mover's truck the day before using red/white tape and a sign with date and hours. Inform your municipality if required.
Mental Preparation	Reduce overwhelm through order and intention.	Recognize that every checklist and label is not just practical but emotional—a way to create calm and readiness for your new chapter.

Chapter 5

Making Moving Day Manageable

And it's here — the big day!

Chances are you went to bed a little later than planned; last-minute packing has a way of stretching time. You've likely woken up bright and early, preparing breakfast and sorting the final few things — like transferring the fridge items into the cooler bag.

Your attire today is purely practical: comfortable clothes and shoes to carry you through a long, active day.

If you haven't already entrusted your "holy of holies" important documents, jewellery, and valuables — to a trusted family member or friend, make sure they're safely packed in your backpack or the special box mentioned in the previous chapter. Mark it clearly with all the coloured tapes, including fragile tape, so it stands out from the rest. That box stays with you and travels in your own car.

You'll also want your go-bag — the one with water, snacks, and essentials for you, your family, and your four-legged companions. If you've arranged for someone to care for your children or pets during the move, they should be arriving soon to pick them up, allowing you to focus on the logistics with a calmer mind.

Keep the payment for the movers ready in an envelope, along with the extra cash you've budgeted for tips and coffee/snack treats. From experience, movers deeply appreciate small gestures of hospitality — a good coffee early on, followed by a snack break two or three hours later, goes a long way.

During my first phase of the move, I hadn't checked which coffee shops opened early, and found myself frantically searching online at dawn. I eventually ordered from one, but the quality left much to be desired. By the second phase, I'd learned my lesson — I'd pre-selected a café with great coffee, called ahead, and arranged delivery for seven coffees that morning. The difference was remarkable: I felt organized, calm, and genuinely enjoyed sharing that small comfort with the team.

The moving truck and the special lift arrived on time and parked neatly in the space I had reserved the day before by cordoning it off with tape and posting a notice. That little bit of preparation paid off immensely — parking in that neighborhood is a daily challenge, so having the space right below the apartment made the process seamless without disrupting traffic.

I was fortunate with my movers this time — easily the best team I've ever worked with. Fast, efficient, practical, and upbeat, they brought an energy that instantly calmed my nerves. They took over the remaining unfinished boxes and got to work. The first move covered the large furniture, older storage boxes, and paintings; the second focused on beds, kitchen appliances, washing machine, and curtains. Watching the lead mover fit everything into the truck was like witnessing a live-action Tetris game — a real-life puzzle master at work.

Once everything was loaded, we took a short snack break before heading off to unload at the new place.

Before leaving, I walked through the apartment one last time, checking cupboards and corners. I had already said my goodbyes, but still paused for a quiet thank you and farewell. I knew I'd be returning the following week when the charity organization was scheduled to collect the remaining items I'd set aside for donation.

Finally, I took a photo of the electricity meter reading, switched off the mains, and closed the door behind me.

And then — off to the new home, where the reserved parking space awaited once more, ready for the unloading to begin.

I ordered another round of coffees from the same café, and by the time they arrived, the unloading was already underway. It's incredible how many boxes there still are — even after decluttering and streamlining your belongings, it somehow still amounts to a small mountain.

The only specific request I made was that the bedroom remain box-free, except for the clothing and towel/linen IKEA storage bags, which went straight into the cupboard shelves. The bedroom, I decided, had to be functional and comfortable from day one — a small haven of calm amidst the sea of boxes.

If you're moving into a large home, you might have enough space to position boxes according to your colour-coded plan. In my case, there wasn't enough room, so the boxes ended up stacked wherever they could fit. Still, I made sure that at least half the lounge area was set up and welcoming — couches and coffee table in place, ready to sit, breathe, or enjoy a simple meal.

The kitchen, though small, had its own charm. It still needed a little table, but until I found the right solution, the coffee table doubled as a dining spot. In those first days, nothing is quite perfect — except for one thing: you're home. And if you have to improvise or use temporary solutions, don't fret. Things fall into place much faster once you begin living in the rhythm of your new space.

Once the movers finished unloading, I paid the owner and tipped each member of the team. They were genuinely pleased — their smiles and good wishes for the new home were a gift in themselves. There was, however, one last task: the swap. I had arranged for them to take my extra couch to my son's godmother and bring back her dining room table. Three of them managed this final exchange, along with delivering a wooden cupboard to a dear family member.

As I've mentioned before, it's always worth asking among family and friends before selling or donating — sometimes the items we no longer need can perfectly serve someone we care about.

When the movers left, I waited for the dining table to arrive. Looking around at the tower of boxes, I felt a mix of exhaustion and relief — the hardest part was over. And underneath it all, a bubbling joy: I was here, in my new home.

This quaint abode, bought with a loan and every ounce of faith (and savings) I could muster, had come to life. There were still improvements to be made, of course, but the major things were done. A deep wave of gratitude rose within me — to life, to Source, for this beautiful blessing.

Whether your new space is rented or bought makes no difference; what truly matters is the love and energy you pour into it. That's what transforms walls into a home.

I walked through each room, quietly sending thoughts of joy, love, and light — gratitude for the shelter, for future gatherings, and for all the beautiful moments yet to unfold here. I encourage you to do the same. Your ritual doesn't have to be elaborate; it only needs one thing — pure intention. See your new home as wonderful, and it will be.

Then, practical me resurfaced. It was time to get organized. Thankfully, I had arranged for professional cleaners the day before, so I could skip the scrubbing and dive straight into the fun part — setting up.

The bathroom was easy-peasy (or should I say pee-easy — pun intended!). I found the clear plastic box, unpacked it into the drawers, set out the new toothbrushes, shampoo, and shower gel, hung the fresh towels, and — voilà — the first room was ready.

Next came the bedroom — time to put on those clean, crisp sheets. I had my fresh pillowcases ready... but alas, couldn't find the pillows. The movers had dismantled the bed and reassembled it beautifully, but it seems they'd tossed the pillows together with the used sheets into a big black garbage bag. I must have been doing something else at the time and hadn't noticed where they'd placed it. There were quite a few such bags piled in awkward spots, difficult to reach.

Eventually, I found the couch cushions and a spare pillow, so I made do for the night. When I finally retrieved the actual pillows, strangely enough, they no longer felt comfortable. I ended up with a stiff neck and went out the next day to buy a new one on sale—only to discover that wasn't comfortable either! So, I've stuck with that trusty spare pillow ever since… go figure.

Lesson learned: when preparing your essential bedding bag for the first night, make sure to add your pillows first thing in the morning. At this stage, I would have also put up the curtains—had I remembered the importance I mentioned in the previous chapter. Bedroom ready!

By then, the dining room table had arrived. I was so happy—it was the perfect size and shape for the room and carried such good, happy karma, having hosted many a delicious meal and lively family gathering.

Then I moved on to the kitchen. The stove/cooker looked so much dirtier than in the previous home—funny how we never see the back and sides of it until moving day! I started cleaning promptly since the electrician was due to arrive—and he did. He installed the stove/cooker, washing machine, and all the light fixtures. I had a large clear plastic box filled with light bulbs of various shapes and strengths—he seemed impressed. He also replaced the on/off switches and plugs.

Once we plugged in the fridge (after giving the refrigerant time to settle), he replaced the broken fridge bulb with a new LED one—new home, new light! He even stuck a small wad of paper under one side of the fridge to stop a wobble caused by the move. It was all quite time-consuming, but worth it.

Finally, it was time for that much-needed first cup of tea. The kettle was in place, and I already had our mugs from the first phase of the move. The food supplies were neatly packed in the big plastic boxes, so unpacking them into the cupboards felt just like putting away a regular grocery shop. Then came the box with the pots and pans—nicely arranged in the lower cupboards, easy to see and reach. Next up were the glasses, though I needed the ladder to reach the upper shelves since they didn't all fit on one.

Soon enough, the kitchen was fairly well organized. I took my well-earned cuppa and went to the lounge to simply be for a little while—tired but happy. So much had taken place to reach this point, and now I felt both relieved and quietly amazed by what had been accomplished. I felt a deep exhale rise from within me — the kind that comes when you've crossed a finish line you once only imagined. There were tons of boxes everywhere, things to sort, small adjustments waiting for their moment, yet everything already felt right. The house, though still in its early stages of becoming a home, was breathing with new energy. Each corner held a whisper of promise, each object a story of care and perseverance. It wasn't just about moving things from one space to another — it was about arriving in a new chapter, one marked by gratitude, light, and the quiet satisfaction of having made it through the day with both heart and humour intact.

Afterwards, I had a quick shower—still thrilled with how lovely the bathroom looked—got dressed, and started to get ready to go my son's godmother's house.

It's in these moments — when the boxes are stacked, the dust is settling, and the adrenaline begins to fade — that you realize how much of a blessing it is to have people in your life who show up when it matters most. Those steady souls who offer calm when everything feels uncertain, who remind you that you're not alone in carrying the load.

My brother was one of those anchors that day. He came by before the movers started to offload, went back to the old apartment to tidy and clean up and throw away what needed to go, and then returned to the new home just before the electrician arrived. His presence alone offered a quiet reassurance — a sense that everything was under control. He was genuinely thrilled for me, almost incredulous that it had all come together. Seeing his happiness and relief mirrored my own. It was a beautiful shared moment — one of those silent exchanges between siblings that says, “You did it... we did it.”

And then, as the evening began to unfold, came another source of comfort and joy — my son’s godmother, my dear friend, chosen family and “village”.

When I arrived at her home, both my son and my four-legged godchild came running out the door, each wanting my full attention. What a lovely, joy-filled reception. My favourite couch looked so perfectly in place there — I was relieved and happy that it had found its new home. Her mum had prepared a delicious meal, and after such a long and eventful day, that warmth and nourishment felt like the ultimate comfort. I had brought dessert, and we all sat together, sharing our thoughts and laughter about the day. My heart was full of gratitude — for the care they had given my precious boy, and for the calm space they created that allowed me to focus on the move.

With hearts and tummies full, it was time to head home.

As I got into bed, I loved the feeling of the clean, fresh sheets and the deep relief of being Home sweet Home.

That's when my son began to cry at the shadows on the wall — and that's exactly why I had stressed the importance of curtains in the previous chapters. After explaining and comforting him, we stepped out onto the balcony to look at the streetlights and passing cars. That's when I realized there was a beautiful quietness — no more motorbikes revving beneath our window — an unexpected blessing of this new space.

We went back inside, and with a smile still plastered on my face and joy overflowing in my heart, it was finally lights out.

The next morning, I was gently woken by sunbeams kissing my cheeks — what a beautiful welcome to the day. It felt like the house itself was greeting us. Too early to get up, I turned around and had a blissful little snooze until my son stirred, asking for breakfast. The kitchen was pretty much organized, and everything flowed with ease

Moving day is rarely perfect — it's often messy, tiring, and full of surprises — but it also carries a sense of achievement, of home coming. It's the moment all the planning, patience, and effort converge into something tangible: the creation of a home. In the end, it's not just about where you've moved, but how you've arrived — with gratitude, love, and a heart open to the light of new beginnings.

Chapter 6

Settling in to Your New Home with Joy

Relax, take a breather — you made it. You are Home!

The very next day, tackle only a few boxes. There will be stacks of them, and that's perfectly fine. Rome wasn't built in a day — just as it took time to pack, it will take perhaps even more time to unpack. Instead, use this first day to decompress. Take a long walk around your new neighborhood, explore the local park, scout for bookshops or try a new coffee shop.

I found one that served the most amazing coffee — a little expensive, but worth every sip — with soft chill-out music playing and sunlight streaming through the windows. It was exactly the calm peace I needed after moving day. My brother brought over a delicious lunch that my sister-in-law had prepared, so I didn't even need to think about cooking.

You need to take care of yourself and your family after such a life-changing event. If you are fortunate to have family and friends who look out for you, now is the time to receive — to allow yourself to be cared for, not always the one giving. If, however, you're far from loved ones, then it's even more important to show kindness to yourself. Take that walk, find a cosy spot – a café, or somewhere to enjoy a meal. These little acts help you feel rooted.

Once home, surround yourself with a few favorite things — an icon, a painting, a photograph of happy times, a lamp casting the right warm hue and softness to add ambience to a room. These are the first touches that transform a space into *your* space.

Life, of course, moves on. The boxes may still be waiting, but the daily routines return — children to school, pets to walk, work to get back to. Go gently, but keep the momentum: one box a day. I unpacked in reverse order — LIFO: last in, first out — starting with the things we needed most.

The furniture and home sometimes dictate where things go… I may have planned for them to be in one spot and have a specific function, but thinking outside the box and seeing that certain things may serve a different purpose in your new home. For example, an antique console table, is now serving as a desk. A carved wooden cabinet that used to be a bookcase is now a place for fine desert plates, serving dishes and cutlery. An old livery cupboard had bric-a-brac that were released in the decluttering phase and now have dinnerware and glasses. Make use of the furniture and nooks you have, especially if you have downsized. As soon as you finished unpacking a box along with bubble packs etc., take it to the recycling bin directly, you feel the difference as the space begins to open up.

Books came last. Despite having given away stacks (and that small encyclopedia incident!), I sifted through them once again and found another two boxes for my dear friend, who is generous in heart and spirit, always ready with words of encouragement and quiet acts of kindness — to take to the charity bazaar.

Even though there were still boxes around and things not quite in place, all my dearest friends still popped by for pizza, dessert, or a quick snack — bringing with them their humour, warmth, and big-hearted support. Connection, I've learned, is one of the essential ingredients for a truly welcoming home.

My son's godmother, her mum, and my four-legged godchild also came to visit. She was growing old and found walking difficult, but she came in my new home wagging her tail even though she was poorly. At one point, she quietly went inside and had a little accident — a small puddle on the floor. We simply laughed and cleaned it up. I chose to see it as her blessing of the house, especially since she passed away a few days later. Our animal companions teach us so much — love without judgement, loyalty without condition. They love us simply as we are, and when they leave our side, their paw prints remain forever in our hearts.

Hanging a painting, placing fresh curtains, positioning a vase, arranging photographs — these are small, joyful acts of settling in. Choose, change, and choose again until it feels right. This is the outer décor of home.

But the true creation of joy begins within. Feel joy, happiness, and light inside you first — because our inner state radiates outward, shaping the energy of the space around us. The keys are intention and emotion. Write down how you wish to feel in your new home — then allow yourself to feel those words.

For example: In my new space, I feel joy, ease, comfort, abundance, peace, happiness, laughter, connection, safety, belonging, kindness, understanding, love, light — and the deep contentment of being Home, not only in a physical sense, but in a soulful, spiritual alignment — a feeling of being centered, whole, and connected to Source.

As I close these pages, I return to the words of Heraclitus — that "everything flows." When I first mentioned them at the beginning of this book, they were a gentle reminder that change is the only constant. Now, standing on the other side of this journey, they have deepened in meaning. For every move, every new beginning, and every letting go is a ripple in the river of life, guiding us toward greater clarity, simplicity, and joy.

We do not resist the current, for that only creates opposition — it is exhausting to think we can control everything. But when we learn to surrender, to go with the flow, to trust, then the beauty, blessings, and lessons unfold naturally. In so doing, we discover that "home" is not only the space we inhabit but also the peace we carry within. Wherever the river of life may take you next — or however many times you move residence — remember to go with that flow; it will always carry you to where you are meant to be.

May your new home, wherever it may be, hold laughter that warms its walls, light that welcomes you each morning, and peace that greets you each night. May you find beauty in the small things — a sunbeam, a shared meal, a quiet moment — and may your heart always know the gentle joy of being Home.

Printed in Dunstable, United Kingdom

75304030R00051